WIRED WORLD

The Rise and Evolution of the Internet

Philipp Frühwirth

CONTENTS

THE PRECURSORS TO THE INTERNET: FROM TELEGRAPHS TO MAINFRAMES

The origins of the internet can be traced back to the telegraph, a device used to transmit messages over long distances using electrical signals. The first telegraph was created in the early 19th century and quickly became an essential tool of communication for businesses and governments around the world.

However, telegraphs were limited in their capabilities and were only able to transmit simple messages in a binary code system. It wasn't until the invention of the telephone in 1876 that communication technology began to evolve beyond the telegraph.

In the early 20th century, the development of the radio and television further expanded the reach of communication technology. Radio broadcasting became a popular way to share news and entertainment, while television revolutionized the way people received visual information and entertainment.

The next significant leap forward in communication technology came with the creation of the first computers in the mid-20th century. These early computers, known as mainframes, were massive machines that filled entire rooms and were used primarily by large organizations and governments for scientific research and data processing.

It was during this time that a breakthrough in networking technology occurred with the creation of the Advanced Research Projects Agency Network (ARPANET). ARPANET was developed in the late 1960s by the United States Department of Defense as a means of communicating with researchers and scientists working on government projects.

ARPANET allowed computers to communicate with each other over long distances by breaking down data into small packets and sending them through a network of interconnected computers. This system of packet switching, as it was called, would become the foundation for the modern internet.

In the 1970s, the birth of personal computers paved the way for the democratization of communication technology. The widespread availability of computers allowed individuals to connect to ARPANET and share information and resources with others.

In conclusion, the precursors to the internet began with the telegraph and continued with the telephone, radio, television, and early computers. The development of ARPANET and packet switching technology would ultimately lead to the creation of the internet as we know it today, allowing people from all over the world to communicate, collaborate, and access information on a massive scale.

THE BIRTH OF THE INTERNET: THE CREATION OF ARPANET

The creation of ARPANET is considered the beginning of the modern Internet. In the late 1960s, the United States Department of Defense's Advanced Research Projects Agency (ARPA) began developing a communication system that connected research institutions and government agencies.

The goal of ARPA was to create a decentralized communication system that could withstand a military attack, and still allow researchers to communicate with one another. By creating a network that was not centralized in one location, they could ensure that the loss of any one computer or communication link would not disrupt the whole network.

In 1969, the first node on the ARPANET was established at UCLA. Soon after, other universities and research institutions, such as Stanford and MIT, joined the network. By the early 1970s, the network had expanded to include various government agencies, such as the Department of Defense and NASA.

The communication method used by the ARPANET was a new technology called packet-switching, which allowed data to be transmitted in small, manageable packets. Instead of sending information in one single stream, this technique divided data into smaller packets which traveled across the network, taking various paths to reach its destination. This ensured that if one part of the network was disrupted or destroyed, the other nodes could still communicate with each other.

The ARPANET also introduced email as a new way of communicating between researchers. The first email message was sent in 1971 by computer engineer Ray Tomlinson, although the contents of that message are unfortunately lost to history.

In conclusion, the creation of the ARPANET laid the groundwork for the Internet we know today. By developing a decentralized communication system that could withstand military attack, researchers and government agencies were able to share information and communicate with one another in a way that was not possible before. The development and expansion of ARPANET was the beginning of a new era of communication and set the stage for the incredible technological advances that have followed.

THE EARLY YEARS OF THE INTERNET: FROM EMAIL TO FILE SHARING

The early years of the internet were characterized by the rise of email and file sharing. In the 1980s, email emerged as a dominant application of the internet, allowing people to communicate with each other instantly across the globe. The first email message, sent by computer engineer Ray Tomlinson in 1971, was a milestone in the history of the internet.

Another key application of the early internet was file sharing, which allowed users to transfer files from one computer to another. Initially, file sharing was done through physical media, such as floppy disks or CDs. However, the emergence of the internet allowed file sharing to be done over computer networks, which greatly increased its functionality and convenience.

One of the most popular file sharing programs of the early internet was Napster, which was founded in 1999. Napster was a peer-to-peer (P2P) file sharing service that allowed users to share music files with each other. The service was hugely popular, with millions of users around the world sharing music files.

However, Napster's success was short-lived, as the service was shut down in 2001 following legal action by the Recording Industry Association of America (RIAA). The RIAA argued that Napster was facilitating illegal distribution of copyrighted material, and the court agreed.

Despite the legal troubles faced by Napster and other file sharing services, file sharing continues to be a popular activity on the internet. Today, there are many popular file sharing services that use P2P technology to allow users to share files of all types, including music, movies, and software.

Overall, the early years of the internet were marked by the emergence of key applications like email and file sharing, which helped to make the internet an accessible and powerful tool for people around the world. While the technology has evolved considerably since then, these early innovations continue to shape the way we use the internet today.

THE WORLD WIDE WEB: THE RISE OF WEB BROWSERS AND HTML

The World Wide Web, also known as the Web, is an essential part of the modern internet. The Web is what most people think of when they think of the internet, a vast network of interconnected documents, images, videos, and other media that are accessed through web browsers. The Web has revolutionized the way we communicate, share information, and conduct business, becoming an essential part of everyday life for billions of people around the world.

The origins of the Web can be traced back to the early 1990s when Tim Berners-Lee, a British computer scientist, developed the first web browser and framework for creating and sharing web pages. Berners-Lee's idea was to make information accessible to anyone, anywhere in the world, regardless of the device, they were using. He called his creation the World Wide Web.

To make the Web accessible, Berners-Lee needed a language that would allow documents to be displayed on any device with an internet connection. He created HyperText Markup Language (HTML), which enabled the creation of web pages and the links between them. HTML allowed users to add images, video, and other media to their documents.

In 1993, Marc Andreessen and Eric Bina created Mosaic, the first web browser with a graphical user interface that made the Web much more accessible to the average person. Mosaic allowed users to see web pages as they would appear on a printed page, and it supported hypertext links, which made it easy to navigate between pages.

The rise of Mosaic and other graphical browsers led to a boom in the development of Web content. Companies began building websites to promote their products and services, and individuals created personal websites to share their interests and hobbies. The Web became a vast repository of information, and search engines like Yahoo! and Google emerged to help users find what they were looking for.

Today, the Web has grown beyond anyone's wildest imagination. There are over 1.7 billion websites on the internet today, with new sites being created every second. The Web has become a vital tool for communication, research, education, entertainment, and much more. It has also become an essential part of many businesses, with e-commerce sites generating trillions of dollars in revenue each year. The Web has changed the world in ways that we are only just beginning to understand, and its future looks even more exciting.

THE DOT-COM BUBBLE: THE RISE AND FALL OF THE FIRST INTERNET BOOM

The late 90s and early 2000s marked the rise of the internet and the dot-com boom. Companies were founded with the sole purpose of establishing a presence on the emerging World Wide Web, and investors flocked to fund online ventures. The dot-com bubble became a period of euphoria and excess, as companies burned through cash while generating little revenue. Companies with no viable business plans and no profits found themselves with massive valuations, and everyone seemed to want a piece of the action.

The bubble came to a head in March 2000 when the NASDAQ peaked and began to decline rapidly. The companies that were once worth billions of dollars were now trading for pennies, and many entrepreneurs and investors went bankrupt almost overnight. The aftermath was sobering, with many businesses failing and thousands of people losing their jobs. The rapid rise and even faster fall of the dot-com industry left many wondering what had gone wrong.

The root causes of the bubble are complex, but several factors contributed to its growth and eventual burst. First, the internet was a new and untested medium, and investors didn't have a clear understanding of how it would generate revenue. Many companies poured huge sums of money into expensive advertising campaigns, hoping to build their brand without considering how they would monetize their services. Second, the availability of venture capital was unprecedented, with investors pouring money into untested startups with little to no oversight. Third, the bubble was stoked by irrational exuberance, as investors and the press hyped up any internet-related story, regardless of how unlikely it was to pan out.

The dot-com bubble was followed by a period of consolidation, where many of the weaker companies went bankrupt or were sold off to stronger competitors. The bubble also had a lasting impact on the way investors view internet companies, with more emphasis placed on solid business plans and revenue growth. Despite the crash, the internet continued to evolve and mature, with new companies emerging to fill the gaps left by the failures of the bubble era.

THE MOBILE REVOLUTION: THE EMERGENCE OF SMARTPHONES AND MOBILE INTERNET

The mobile revolution began in 2007 with the introduction of the first iPhone by tech giant Apple. The iPhone was not just another digital device but a transformative product that would kickstart the mobile revolution. The iPhone was the first device of its kind, and it quickly became a sensation. A year later, Google introduced Android devices, which further fueled the growth of the mobile revolution.

The mobile revolution was marked by the creation of a new market: the smartphone market. The market grew rapidly, and soon, smartphones became an essential part of our daily lives. Almost everyone today owns a smartphone, and for most people, it is their primary device for accessing the internet.

Smartphones are the most popular way of accessing the internet today. The convenience of carrying around a device that can surf the web, send email, and make calls is unmatched. With the advent of smartphones, the internet became a mobile experience, allowing users to access information anywhere they are. Today, mobile devices account for almost two-thirds of all internet traffic.

With the mobile revolution came a massive shift in how websites are designed. Websites that were once built for large screens were now being viewed on small mobile screens. This meant that websites had to be redesigned to fit smaller screens, and new technologies and standards had to be developed to help create mobile-friendly web pages. The introduction of HTML5 was one such development that enabled web developers to create websites that were optimized for mobile devices.

The mobile revolution has also transformed the way we shop, bank, and communicate. Mobile payments have become more popular, allowing people to pay for goods and services using their smartphones. With mobile banking, people can make transactions and check their balances on the go. Mobile communication has also become easier and more convenient, with options like messaging, email, and video conferencing all available on a single device.

In conclusion, the mobile revolution changed the way we access the internet, communicate, and conduct transactions. It turned the smartphone into an essential tool for modern life and created new opportunities for businesses to reach customers. The future of the mobile revolution is exciting, with new technologies like 5G and upcoming foldable screens set to bring even more radical changes to the mobile landscape.

WEB 2.0: SOCIAL MEDIA, USER-GENERATED CONTENT, AND ONLINE COLLABORATION

The evolution of the internet continued with the advent of Web 2.0, which marked the introduction of user-generated content and online collaboration. Before Web 2.0, the internet was largely static, with content created and controlled by a small group of webmasters. However, the rise of social media, blogs, and other user-generated content platforms have completely changed the way we perceive and interact with the internet.

In the early 2000s, social networking sites such as Friendster and MySpace began to emerge, allowing people to create their profiles and connect with others online. This allowed users to share their thoughts, opinions, and media with a broader audience, and paved the way for the rise of platforms like Facebook and Twitter, which continue to change the way we communicate and interact with each other.

Blogs also became a widespread platform for publishing content online, with platforms like WordPress and Blogger making it easier than ever for anyone to start a blog. Blogging allowed people to publish their writing, photography, and other creative works online, providing a new level of accessibility and democratization for online publishing.

Online collaboration platforms, such as Google Docs and Dropbox, also emerged, allowing groups to work on documents, presentations, and other projects in real-time. This made it easier for remote teams to work together, and to share their work with others regardless of their location.

Another crucial aspect of Web 2.0 was the emergence of platforms, such as YouTube, Flickr, and SoundCloud, which allowed users to share their media content with the wider online community. This enabled the creation of an online culture of sharing, where users could access and consume content created by others, and also contribute their own work for others to see.

Web 2.0 has enabled a new level of interaction with the internet, transforming it from a static platform to an ever-evolving and engaging resource. Today, billions of people use social media, blogs, and other online platforms to express their ideas, share perspectives, and collaborate with others across the globe.

E-COMMERCE: THE GROWTH OF ONLINE SHOPPING AND DIGITAL MARKETPLACES

E-commerce, or electronic commerce, refers to commercial transactions that are conducted online. This includes buying and selling goods and services, as well as transferring funds electronically. Over the years, e-commerce has become an increasingly important part of the global economy, with more and more people turning to online shopping and digital marketplaces.

The history of e-commerce dates back to the early days of the internet. In the 1990s, a number of e-commerce sites began to emerge, such as Amazon and eBay, offering consumers the ability to purchase goods and services online. Back then, the process was still clunky and required a lot of trust in the sellers, but it was clear that there was immense potential for e-commerce.

As the internet and technology continued to advance, so too did e-commerce. Digital payment platforms such as PayPal and Square emerged, making it easier and more secure to conduct transactions online. This led to an explosion in the number of online retailers, with companies of all sizes turning to e-commerce as a way to reach new customers and expand their businesses.

One of the key benefits of e-commerce is its convenience. Customers can shop from anywhere at any time, without ever having to leave their homes. This has led to the rise of digital marketplaces, such as Amazon and Alibaba, that offer a wide range of products from a variety of sellers all in one place.

Another benefit of e-commerce is its ability to reach a global audience. With the internet, companies can sell to customers all over the world, breaking down physical barriers and opening up new markets.

However, e-commerce has also faced challenges, particularly in the area of security. With so much sensitive information being exchanged online, there is always a risk of identity theft and fraud. Companies must take steps to ensure the security of their customers' data, including encryption and other forms of protection.

Overall, e-commerce has had a profound impact on the way we shop and do business. As technology continues to advance, it is likely that e-commerce will only become more important, with new innovations and opportunities emerging in the digital space.

ONLINE ADVERTISING: FROM BANNER ADS TO TARGETED ADS AND ADTECH

Online advertising has come a long way since the first banner ad appeared online in 1994. It has become an integral part of the digital economy, with annual spending reaching more than $300 billion worldwide. Today, online advertising is a sophisticated industry, employing advanced targeting technologies and data analytics to deliver personalized advertising to consumers.

The early days of online advertising were marked by static banner ads, which were placed on websites as a way to generate revenue. These ads were often intrusive, annoying to users, and had low click-through rates. However, they paved the way for more sophisticated display ads, which became prevalent in the early 2000s. Display ads were more visually appealing and incorporated more interactive elements, such as animation and video.

As the number of websites increased, so did the need for more targeted advertising. In the mid-2000s, the advent of ad networks allowed advertisers to reach a wider audience across multiple websites. Ad networks enabled advertisers to target consumers based on demographic information, such as age and location. However, this approach was limited by the fact that ad networks could only collect data from the websites they served ads on.

The rise of social media platforms brought about a new era in online advertising. Social media sites such as Facebook and Twitter allowed advertisers to use the vast amount of data they collected from users to deliver highly targeted ads. Advertisers could target users based on their interests, behaviors, and even their friend networks. This led to the development of programmatic advertising, which uses algorithms to automate the buying and selling of online ads in real-time.

Today, online advertising is dominated by a few large players, such as Google and Facebook, who have built complex ad networks that reach billions of users. These networks use sophisticated targeting techniques, such as retargeting and lookalike modeling, to deliver highly personalized ads. Advertisers can also take advantage of advanced analytics tools, such as Google Analytics and Adobe Analytics, to measure the effectiveness of their campaigns and optimize their ad spend.

While online advertising has come a long way since the early days of banner ads, it still faces challenges such as ad fraud and data privacy concerns. As the industry continues to evolve and grow, it will need to find ways to balance the needs of advertisers with the rights of users to control their data and online experience.

THE DARK WEB: THE HIDDEN UNDERBELLY OF THE INTERNET

The internet is like an iceberg: what we see – the websites, social media platforms, and search engines – only represents a small part of the immense and complex network that makes up the web. Below the surface, there's a vast and obscure underbelly known as the Dark Web, where anonymity, secrecy, and illegal activities thrive.

What is the Dark Web?
The Dark Web is a part of the internet that is not indexed by standard search engines, and therefore, not accessible through regular browsers like Firefox, Chrome, or Safari. Instead, you need to use a specific anonymizing browser, such as Tor, I2P, or Freenet, to access the Dark Web.

Unlike the surface web, the content on the Dark Web is not openly available and is hidden behind layers of encryption and privacy tools. It's used by dissidents, political activists, journalists, and individuals who want to communicate or browse the web anonymously, without leaving any digital trail. While some of these individuals have legitimate reasons to hide their identity, much of the content that exists on the Dark Web is illegal in nature.

What Goes on in the Dark Web?
One of the main attractions of the Dark Web is that it provides a safe haven for all kinds of illegal activities, including drug trafficking, weapons trading, counterfeit documents, hacking services, stolen data, and child pornography, to name a few. These activities are facilitated by anonymous marketplaces, such as Silk Road, AlphaBay, and Dream Market, where vendors and buyers can

transact in cryptocurrencies and remain untraceable.

The Dark Web is also a hub for cybercriminals and hacking groups who sell their services to the highest bidder on the black market. These services include distributed denial-of-service (DDoS) attacks, malware infections, phishing scams, and ransomware, which can cause severe damages to individuals, organizations, and entire governments.

The Risks of the Dark Web
Accessing the Dark Web can be very dangerous, especially for those who are not careful about their online activity. Many of the websites on the Dark Web are designed to spread malware, steal personal information, or scam unsuspecting users. There are no regulations, customer protection laws or legal recourse available if something goes wrong.

Furthermore, accessing or participating in illegal activities on the Dark Web can have serious legal consequences. Law enforcement agencies are always on the lookout for criminal activity on the Dark Web and have been successful in shutting down marketplaces and arresting cybercriminals.

In Conclusion
While the Dark Web might seem like an exciting and mysterious place to explore, it's important to remember that it's not a safe or legally sanctioned part of the internet. Users who venture into the Dark Web need to be aware of the risks and take appropriate precautions to avoid harm.

CYBERSECURITY: THE CONSTANT BATTLE AGAINST ONLINE THREATS AND CYBERATTACKS

As the internet has evolved to become an integral part of our daily lives, it has also become a target for cybercriminals seeking to exploit vulnerabilities in the system. Cybersecurity has become a crucial issue for individuals, businesses, and governments as the frequency and complexity of cyberattacks continue to increase. In this chapter, we will explore the history of cybersecurity and the measures taken to combat online threats.

The first recorded computer virus was created in 1971 by a programmer named Bob Thomas. The virus, called Creeper, was an experimental game that spread easily through ARPANET but caused no real damage. A few years later, in 1979, the first major cyberattack occurred when an intruder named Kevin Mitnick gained unauthorized access to the computer network at the University of Southern California. From then on, cyberattacks have become increasingly more sophisticated and harmful.

The rise of the internet and networking technologies have led to a new generation of threats such as malware, phishing, ransomware, and other types of attacks. These attacks can take different forms such as denial of service (DoS) attacks, stealing sensitive data, espionage, and botnets. By leveraging loopholes in software, social engineering techniques, and other methods, cybercriminals are able to bypass various security measures and cause significant damages.

To combat these threats, various organizations and governments have implemented policies and measures to enhance cybersecurity. The first computer security legislation was passed in 1984 with the Computer Fraud and Abuse Act in the United States. This was followed by other policies such as the Federal Information Security Management Act (FISMA) and the Cybersecurity Information Sharing Act (CISA), which aimed to promote secure communication and collaboration between government and private entities.

Additionally, cybersecurity has seen significant growth in the private sector. Companies have been developing new tools, including firewalls, intrusion detection and prevention software, and security information and event management (SIEM) solutions, which use Artificial Intelligence (AI) and Machine Learning algorithms to detect and respond to threats in real-time.

In summary, cybersecurity has become a vital issue in the digital era, and efforts to boost online safety continue to evolve. With the advancement of technology and the ever-growing use of the internet, it is crucial to be mindful of the risks and take appropriate measures to prevent criminal activities that undermine the security of our digital world.

THE INTERNET OF THINGS: THE NEXT FRONTIER OF CONNECTED DEVICES

The Internet of Things (IoT) refers to the network of interconnected devices that can collect, exchange, and analyze data without human intervention. This technology has been rising in popularity in recent years due to the increased demand for automation and the integration of smart devices into daily life.

IoT devices range from simple sensors to sophisticated machines that are equipped with sensors, software, and data storage components. These devices can be found in various industries, such as healthcare, transportation, manufacturing, and smart homes.

The benefits of IoT include improved efficiency, cost savings, and enhanced user experiences. For example, in manufacturing, IoT devices can help detect faults in machines before they become critical, resulting in less downtime and reduced maintenance costs. In the healthcare industry, IoT devices can help monitor patients remotely, providing personalized care and reducing the need for hospitalization.

However, the rise of the IoT also presents significant security risks. IoT devices are often unsecured and can be vulnerable to cyber-attacks. The lack of regulations and standards in the IoT industry makes it difficult to implement proper security measures, leaving devices open to exploitation.

To address these concerns, IoT manufacturers and service providers are incorporating security features into their devices, such as encryption, authentication, and access control.

Governments are also adopting regulations and standards for IoT devices to ensure their security, reliability, and privacy.

The future of the IoT is also exciting, with the integration of artificial intelligence (AI) and machine learning (ML) into IoT devices. This will enable devices to learn from past experiences and make more accurate predictions, providing better insights and enhancing automation. The use of 5G networks will also improve the connectivity and speed of IoT devices, opening up new opportunities for innovation and growth.

In conclusion, the IoT is a promising technology that presents numerous benefits but also significant security challenges. As the number of IoT devices continues to grow, implementing effective security measures will be crucial to prevent unwanted access and ensure privacy. The IoT also provides a vast opportunity for innovation and growth, and its impact on society and industries is expected to continue to increase in the coming years.

CLOUD COMPUTING: THE FUTURE OF DATA STORAGE AND PROCESSING

With the increasing amount of data generated by businesses, governments and individuals, the need for efficient and cost-effective data storage solutions has become crucial. This is where cloud computing comes in. Cloud computing is a technology that allows businesses and individuals to store and access data and software applications over the internet rather than on a physical device. With cloud computing, data can be stored on remote servers and accessed from anywhere with an internet connection.

Cloud computing has several advantages over traditional data storage methods. Firstly, it provides businesses with flexibility and scalability in terms of storage space. As the amount of data a business generates grows, it can simply adjust the amount of storage space it requires without having to invest in additional hardware or infrastructure. This can result in substantial cost savings.

Secondly, cloud computing allows for greater collaboration and accessibility. With all data stored in the cloud, authorized users can access it from anywhere, at any time, through any device. This promotes greater collaboration and efficiency among teams regardless of their location.

Thirdly, cloud computing provides businesses with enhanced security measures. Cloud providers offer reliable backup and disaster recovery services that protect data in case of a natural disaster or cyber attack. Additionally, cloud providers typically offer robust security measures such as encryption, identity management, and network segmentation to protect data from unauthorized access.

There are three main types of cloud computing services:

1. Infrastructure as a Service (IaaS) - this allows businesses to rent infrastructure such as servers, storage, and networking on a pay-per-use basis.

2. Software as a Service (SaaS) - this allows businesses to rent software applications such as email, collaboration software, or sales and marketing software, on a pay-per-use basis.

3. Platform as a Service (PaaS) - this allows businesses to rent hosted development environments on which they can create, test, and deploy software applications.

Cloud computing has emerged as a game changer in the world of data storage and processing. The convenience, scalability, flexibility, and cost-effectiveness of cloud computing coupled with robust security measures make the technology appealing to businesses and individuals alike. As more businesses and organizations opt for cloud computing solutions, the trend of data being stored and accessed from a remote location is set to become the norm.

BIG DATA: THE RISE OF DATA ANALYTICS AND MACHINE LEARNING

Over the last decade, big data has revolutionized how businesses and organizations analyze and interpret large and complex sets of data. Big data refers to the collection, storage, and analysis of massive amounts of data.

This innovation has been made possible by the creation of new technologies such as data analytics and machine learning. Data analytics is the process of examining large and complex data sets to identify patterns, correlations and other insights that businesses can use to make informed decisions. Machine learning, on the other hand, focuses on the development of algorithms that can learn and make predictions on data.

One of the biggest challenges when it comes to big data is the sheer volume of information that needs to be processed. The traditional tools and technologies that were used to analyze data were not equipped to handle this volume and complexity of data. However, with the growth of cloud computing and advanced platforms like Hadoop, businesses can now collect, store and analyze this data in real-time.

The rise of big data has had a significant impact on various industries, ranging from healthcare to finance. For example, in healthcare, big data has enabled medical professionals to analyze patient data to provide better diagnoses and treatment. In the finance industry, big data has helped banks and other financial institutions to assess risks and fraud, and identify profitable investments.

With the growth of machine learning, big data is now being used to develop more advanced artificial intelligence (AI) systems. Machine learning is being used to develop systems that can understand human language, recognize patterns in images, and make predictions based on data. These technologies are already being used in applications like voice recognition, virtual assistants, and self-driving cars.

However, despite the huge potential of big data and machine learning, there are still concerns around data privacy and security. As businesses collect and analyze more data about their customers, there is a risk that this information could be used unethically or fall into the wrong hands. As a result, it's essential for businesses to prioritize data privacy and security to ensure that big data is used ethically and responsibly.

In conclusion, big data and machine learning have revolutionized how businesses process and analyze data. With the potential to transform industries and pave the way for more advanced AI, big data is set to remain a vital component of the technological landscape for years to come. However, we must ensure that we use this technology responsibly and prioritize data privacy and security.

VIRTUAL REALITY AND AUGMENTED REALITY: THE FUTURE OF IMMERSIVE EXPERIENCES ONLINE

Virtual and augmented reality are technologies that have been around for decades, but only recently have they become accessible and practical for everyday use thanks to advancements in hardware and software. These technologies are revolutionizing the way we experience the world, and are opening up new possibilities in entertainment, education, and even medicine.

Virtual Reality (VR) is a technology that creates a fully immersive, three-dimensional computer-generated environment. Using a VR headset, users can physically move around, interact with objects, and feel as though they are actually inside the virtual world. VR has been used primarily in gaming, with many companies creating games and experiences specifically for the technology. VR technology has also been used in education, training, and therapy applications.

Augmented Reality (AR), on the other hand, overlays digital information onto the real world. This could be as simple as a filter that adds cat ears and whiskers to a selfie, or as complex as an AR-powered instruction manual that highlights the steps of a process on the actual product. AR has also been used for education and training, as well as in marketing and advertising campaigns.

The potential applications of VR and AR are limitless, and many industries are exploring the possibilities. For example, the medical field is using VR to simulate surgical procedures and train medical professionals, while AR is being used to aid surgeons with navigating complex surgeries.

In the entertainment industry, VR and AR are opening up new possibilities for storytelling and experiencing media. Hollywood studios are creating VR experiences to accompany blockbuster films, while video game companies are using VR to create fully immersive gaming experiences.

One of the most exciting prospects of VR and AR is their potential to revolutionize workplace collaboration. With remote work becoming more common, VR and AR can allow for virtual meetings, conferences, and collaborations that truly make it feel like everyone is in the same room. This could create a more efficient and collaborative way of working across long distances.

Overall, VR and AR are rapidly evolving technologies with the potential to change the way we interact with the world. As the technology advances and becomes more accessible, we can expect to see many more exciting developments and applications in the years to come.

ONLINE GAMING: THE GLOBAL INDUSTRY OF VIDEO GAMES AND ESPORTS

Video games have been popular for decades, but they truly rocketed to the forefront of mainstream entertainment with the emergence of online gaming. With the rise of personal computers and the internet came the ability to connect to other gamers around the world, and the industry has never been the same.

Online gaming has become a global phenomenon, with millions of players logging on to compete and cooperate with each other on a daily basis. Online games can be played across a range of platforms, including personal computers, consoles, and mobile devices.

One of the biggest draws of online gaming is the ability to play with others in massive multiplayer games, such as World of Warcraft, Final Fantasy XIV, and Guild Wars 2. These games can support thousands of players in the same virtual world simultaneously, leading to truly massive social experiences that connect people from all over the world.

In addition to massively multiplayer games, online gaming also includes competitive e-sports, where the best players in the world compete in organized tournaments with huge cash prizes. E-sports have exploded in popularity in recent years and are now broadcast on major television networks and streamed online to millions of viewers.

The online gaming industry is a massive business, with billions of dollars in revenue generated each year. Game developers and publishers are constantly developing new titles, expanding existing games, and releasing new downloadable content to keep players engaged and entertained.

Online gaming has also brought new innovation to the industry, with advancements such as virtual reality, augmented reality, and cloud gaming. The ability to stream games directly from servers rather than requiring players to install and run them on their own devices has the potential to revolutionize the industry even further.

While online gaming has had its fair share of controversies, from concerns over addiction to issues with online harassment and cyberbullying, it has undeniably transformed the way we play and experience video games. With the industry showing no signs of slowing down, online gaming is set to remain a major force in the entertainment world for years to come.

THE SHARING ECONOMY: FROM AIRBNB TO UBER, HOW THE INTERNET CHANGED THE WAY WE TRAVEL AND WORK

The advent of the Internet has changed the way we live our lives, and nowhere is that more apparent than in the sharing economy. The sharing economy is a system of peer-to-peer transactions where individuals share access to goods and services with each other, rather than owning them themselves. This has given rise to a number of new businesses that have revolutionized the way we travel and work, including Airbnb and Uber.

Airbnb is a platform that allows people to rent out their homes, apartments, or spare rooms to travelers. This has enabled travelers to experience the local culture in a more authentic and affordable way, while also providing a way for hosts to earn extra income. Since its launch in 2008, Airbnb has grown to operate in over 220 countries and has over 7 million property listings worldwide.

Uber is a ride-hailing service that connects passengers with drivers through a smartphone app. This has disrupted the traditional taxi industry, providing a more convenient and reliable way for people to get around. Uber operates in over 700 cities worldwide and has over 110 million monthly active users.

The sharing economy has also given rise to other businesses such as TaskRabbit, a platform that connects people with local freelancers to complete small tasks, and Zipcar, a car-sharing service that allows people to rent cars on a short-term basis.

The sharing economy has had a significant impact on the way we travel and work. It has given travelers more options and flexibility, while also providing hosts and entrepreneurs with new ways to earn income. However, it has also raised concerns about safety, regulation, and the impact on traditional industries.

One of the main criticisms of the sharing economy is that it operates in a regulatory grey area. Many of these services operate outside traditional industry regulations, which can lead to safety concerns for both hosts and guests. There have also been concerns about the impact of the sharing economy on traditional industries, such as hotels and taxis. Some have argued that the rise of Airbnb and Uber has led to a decline in business for these industries.

Despite these concerns, the sharing economy is here to stay. As more people become connected to the Internet and as technology continues to advance, we can expect to see further innovation in this space. The sharing economy has fundamentally changed the way we travel and work, and it will continue to shape our lives in the years to come.

THE FUTURE OF WORK: REMOTE WORK, FREELANCING, AND THE GIG ECONOMY

The internet has facilitated several transformative changes in the job market. One of these changes is the rise of remote work, freelancing, and the gig economy. Thanks to the internet, people can now work from anywhere in the world, build a career on their terms, and have more control over their lives.

Remote work has been made possible by a combination of factors. In the past, the tools to collaborate and communicate remotely were too expensive and too complex for most organizations. But now, with the internet, you can work with team members across the globe using collaboration tools such as Slack, Zoom, and Trello.

At the same time, freelancing has become more and more popular in recent years. The internet has created new opportunities for freelancers to find work on a project-by-project basis. Platforms such as Upwork, Fiverr, and Freelancer have exploded in popularity, connecting businesses with freelancers from all over the world.

The gig economy is a new phenomenon made possible by the internet. Platforms like Uber, Lyft, and Airbnb have revolutionized the transportation and accommodation industries, allowing people to work as drivers or rent out their homes or apartments.

The future of work will continue to be shaped by the internet. More industries will adopt remote work as the norm, and more people will be attracted to the flexibility and autonomy it offers.

Freelancing will become more widespread and will become a viable career option for more people. We will also see more gig-economy platforms emerge, offering a variety of services to consumers.

However, with these innovations come new challenges. Working remotely can be isolating and may blur the lines between work and personal life. Freelancers may face difficulties getting paid on time, and the gig economy has led to controversy over labor laws and worker protections.

To ensure that the future of work benefits everyone, policymakers, employers, and workers must work together to address these challenges. The internet has unlocked new levels of flexibility and opportunity in the workplace, and by taking steps to address the associated challenges, we can ensure that the future of work is one that benefits all.

THE ROLE OF THE INTERNET IN POLITICS: FROM ONLINE CAMPAIGNS TO CYBERWARFARE

The internet has had a revolutionary effect on political campaigns and electioneering. Before the rise of the internet, political campaigns were run on traditional media, such as television, radio, and newspapers. However, with the advent of the internet, political campaigns can reach a wider audience, recruit volunteers, and solicit donations from supporters.

Online campaigning has become more common in recent years. Candidates and parties use email, social media, and other online platforms to connect with supporters, broadcast their message, and attract new voters. They can now target specific demographics, such as millennials or Hispanics, with ads and posts that resonate with these groups.

One of the main advantages of online campaigning is the ease of communication. Supporters can easily share information, ideas, and opinions with candidates or like-minded individuals without having to attend rallies or events. Social media platforms like Twitter and Facebook have become essential tools for political candidates, who can share their viewpoints and engage with voters on key issues.

However, the internet has also created new challenges for political campaigns, such as cybersecurity threats and disinformation campaigns. Hackers can target campaigns to steal information or launch cyber-attacks. Social media can be used to spread fake news, propaganda, and other disinformation, which can influence public opinion and impact the outcome of elections.

The role of the internet in politics also extends to government activities, such as surveillance and cyberwarfare. Governments around the world have used the internet to spy on foreign powers, monitor their own citizens, and even launch cyber-attacks against other countries. Internet censorship and restrictions have also become a major issue in some countries, where governments control internet access or block certain websites and social media platforms.

In conclusion, the internet has had a transformative effect on the way political campaigns are run and on government activities, both domestically and internationally. While online campaigning offers many advantages, it also creates new threats that need to be addressed to ensure the integrity of the democratic process and protect national security.

THE NEXT FRONTIER: THE EVOLUTION OF THE INTERNET AND WHAT'S NEXT FOR THE WORLD WIDE WEB.

The internet has come a long way since its inception, from just connecting military and academic computers to becoming a ubiquitous presence in our daily lives. The World Wide Web has become the primary tool for communication, entertainment, and commerce, as well as a platform for innovation and collaboration.

But what's next for the internet? What are the new technologies and trends that will shape the future of the World Wide Web? Let's explore some of the possible directions that the internet might take in the years to come.

1. Artificial intelligence: The rise of machine learning and artificial intelligence is set to transform the internet, making it more personalized, intuitive, and efficient. AI-powered systems will be able to learn from our behavior and adapt to our preferences, creating more personalized and relevant experiences for each user.

2. Blockchain technology: Blockchain technology has the potential to revolutionize the internet by providing a decentralized platform for secure and transparent transactions. Blockchain-powered systems can eliminate the need for intermediaries, reduce fraud and corruption, and increase trust between parties.

3. 5G networks: The rollout of 5G networks promises to bring faster internet speeds, lower latency, and greater capacity,

enabling new applications and services that were previously impossible. The increased bandwidth will also facilitate the growth of IoT devices and the expansion of the sharing economy.

4. Virtual and augmented reality: VR and AR will continue to grow and gain mainstream adoption, enabling immersive experiences for gaming, education, and training. As the technology advances, it may also transform how we communicate, work, and socialize online.

5. Quantum computing: Quantum computing is poised to revolutionize the internet by providing unprecedented computational power and speed. Quantum computers can solve complex problems that traditional computers cannot, and they may be used to develop new encryption methods and improve data processing and analysis.

6. Improved privacy and security: As the internet becomes more interconnected and data-driven, privacy and security concerns become more pressing. New technologies and policies will need to be developed to ensure the protection of personal information and prevent malicious attacks and data breaches.

7. Green internet: The growth of the internet has led to an increase in energy consumption and carbon emissions. New technologies and policies will need to be developed to make the internet more energy-efficient and sustainable.

The future of the internet and the World Wide Web is full of exciting possibilities and challenges. As these new technologies and trends emerge, it is up to us to shape them in a way that benefits everyone and helps us build a more connected, innovative, and equitable world.

www.ingramcontent.com/pod-product-compliance
Lightning Source LLC
Chambersburg PA
CBHW071145220526
45467CB00015B/1951